**FRIENDS
OF ACPL**

UG 1 1 2004   P9-DZA-268

That Blessed Christmas Night

Dori Chaconas

Illustrated by
Deborah Perez-Stable

Abingdon Press
Nashville

That Blessed Christmas Night

Scripture quotations noted NIV are taken from the HOLY BIBLE, NEW INTERNATIONAL VERSION®. Copyright © 1973, 1978, 1984 by International Bible Society. Used by permission of Zondervan Publishing House. All rights reserved.

ISBN 0-687-00626-0

04 05 06 07 08 09 10 11 12 13—10 9 8 7 6 5 4 3 2 1

Manufactured in China

For all my lovely aunts—
Julia, Julie, Cecelia, Judy, Betty, Anne, Verna, Helen, Priscilla and Lee—
With Love,
Dori

For my dad, aka Grandpa Duck,
with loving thanks for years of Christmas light, music, and joy.

With special thanks to the stars—
Alex, Robert, Noah, Jordan, Tessa, Maddie, Tucker, Audrey,
Jessie, Ben, Coleen, Kasey, Calvin, and Clare

Deborah

For we are God's workmanship, created in Christ Jesus to do good works,
which God prepared in advance for us to do.

Ephesians 2:10

The stars were shining, oh, so bright,
Like glowing diamonds, clear and white,
Sending down their golden light,
That blessed Christmas night.

Near Bethlehem, a Child was born,

Inside a stable, old and worn,

Before the night turned into morn,

That blessed Christmas night.

Oh! How the angels sang!
They sang their songs of glory.
They sang the praises of the Child—
The holy Christmas story.

The Babe was such a tiny thing!

Did he hear the angels sing?

Did he hear their music ring?

That blessed Christmas night.

Shepherds watched their flocks with care.
Then angel voices filled the air,
To tell them of the Child so fair,
That blessed Christmas night.

The shepherds went, with all their sheep,

And found the Infant fast asleep,

In a manger, safe and deep,

That blessed Christmas night.

And in that poor and lowly place,

A gentle smile warmed Mary's face,

Full of tenderness and grace,

That blessed Christmas night.

Oh! How the angels sang!
They sang their songs of glory.
They sang the praises of the Child—
The holy Christmas story.

Joseph watched, so kind and wise,
Adored the Child with loving eyes,
Protective of his tiny size,
That blessed Christmas night.

A snow white dove, in rafters high,
Watched the Babe with soulful sigh.
She cooed a soft, sweet lullaby.
That blessed Christmas night.

The donkey with his coat of gray,
Was pleased that he could share his hay.
He did not bellow, did not bray,
That blessed Christmas night.

The gentle cow, with coat of red,
Knelt down beside the Baby's bed.
The softest "moo" was all she said.
That blessed Christmas night.

Oh! How the angels sang!
They sang their songs of glory.
They sang the praises of the Child—
The holy Christmas story.

And, oh! How we sing along,

This holy, blessed praising song.

Our voices ring across the earth,

In celebration of his birth.

We sing of Christ, our Lord, our Light.

We sing this blessed Christmas night.